# Contents

KU-520-226

Some words are printed in bold, **like this**. You can find out what they mean on page 30. You can also look in the box at the bottom of the page where they first appear.

# Sailing the oceans

Sailing across an ocean is easy in a modern ship. Ships have powerful engines that take the ship wherever it needs to go.

**Satellites** also help ships. Satellites are machines that circle high above the Earth. Some satellites tell the captain where the ship is. Other satellites watch the weather. They send weather reports to the ship. These reports help the captain to **forecast** if the weather is going to change.

Three hundred years ago ships did not have powerful engines. They only had sails. They could not go anywhere unless the wind was blowing. There were no satellites. Sailors had to forecast the weather. They did this by watching the clouds and feeling which way the wind was blowing.

And on top of all this, they had to watch out for pirates!

**forecast**   work out what will happen in the future
**satellite**   machine circling in space above the Earth

▲ This is a modern weather satellite. Satellites make it easier for us to forecast the weather correctly.

# An offshore wind

So, how would you like to travel on a sailing ship from the 1700s? The trip will have to start in the evening. In the evenings there is often an **offshore wind**. This means that the wind is blowing from the land to the sea.

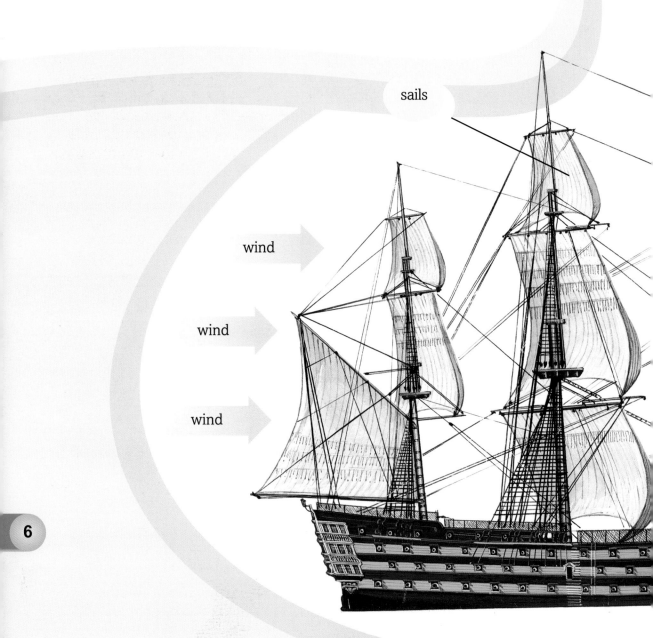

sails

wind

wind

wind

During the day, there is often a wind blowing from the sea towards the land. This is called an **onshore wind**. You can find out why on the next page.

◀ *In the 1700s, there were no engines on ships. Ships needed wind to make them move. The sails caught the wind. The power of the wind made the ship move forwards in the water.*

**offshore wind**   wind blowing from the land out to sea
**onshore wind**   wind blowing from the sea towards the land

# Land and sea breezes

The warmth of the Sun is the main reason why winds blow. During the daytime, the Sun heats the Earth. Land warms up faster than the sea. The air over the land gets warm faster than the air over the sea. Warm air rises. Cooler air then blows in from the sea. It takes the place of the rising warm air. There is an **onshore wind**.

At night the land cools more quickly than the sea. In the evening the air over the sea is warmer than the air over the land. The warmer air rises. Cooler air blows from the land. It takes the place of the rising warm air. There is an **offshore wind**.

It is fine weather as your ship sails out of the harbour. But what will it be like in the morning?

These diagrams show ▶ how onshore and offshore winds work.

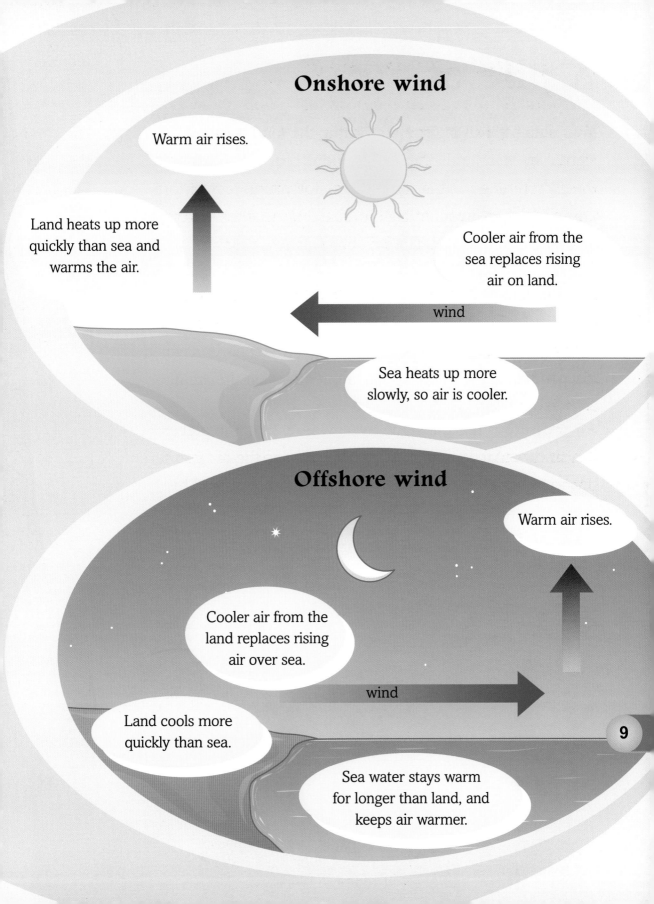

# A pile of air

Your ship sails all night. By morning the land is out of sight. The weather is fine. The wind is blowing the ship in the right direction. It is a good time for you to learn more about weather **forecasting**. Forecasting weather means being able to tell what the weather will do.

The Earth is covered by a layer of air. This layer is called the **atmosphere**. The weight of the atmosphere presses down on the Earth. The weight of the atmosphere is called **air pressure**. Air pressure has a big effect on the weather.

Air pressure is not the same everywhere. In some places the air is warm. Warm air rises. This makes the air pressure lower. In other places the air is cool. Cool air sinks. This makes the air pressure higher.

**air pressure**  weight of the layer of air around the Earth
**atmosphere**  layer of air around the Earth

▼This photo of the Earth's atmosphere was taken in space. The blue lines are the atmosphere. It is thousands of kilometres thick. You can see the Moon in the distance.

*Stormy weather is ▲
caused by very low
air pressure.*

# Stormy weather

It is the first afternoon of your sea journey. You look ahead. You see a dark shape in the distance. Is it land? No, it is storm clouds!

Soon the waves grow bigger. It gets dark as the storm clouds rush towards the ship. Rain starts falling. The wind becomes stronger and stronger.

Winds blow because of differences in **air pressure**. Air rushes away from places where the air pressure is high. Air moves to places where the air pressure is low. Air rushes more quickly into places where air pressure is very low. This can cause very strong winds called **gales**.

## Air pressure watch

*A barometer is used to measure air pressure. It can be used to **forecast** the weather. This means it can tell us if the weather will change. The weather is usually fine when the air pressure is high. If the air pressure becomes low, it means that rain is on the way.*

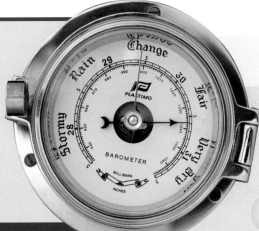

13

**gale**  very strong wind

# South and then west

Your ship is sailing across the Atlantic Ocean from Europe to North America. The shortest route would be to sail west. But ships sailing to North America from Europe always started by sailing south.

The ships sailed south until they reached the **tropics**. The tropics are the warm parts on either side of the **Equator**.

The winds usually blow from east to west in the tropics. This makes it easier and quicker to sail west.

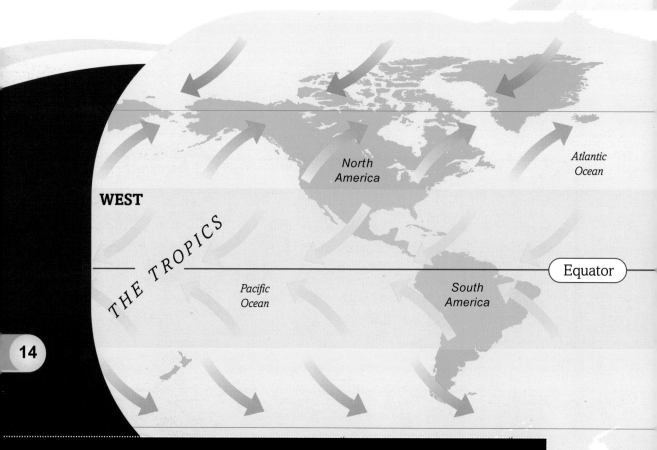

WEST

THE TROPICS

North America

Atlantic Ocean

Pacific Ocean

South America

Equator

**Equator**          imaginary line around the middle of the Earth
**prevailing wind**  direction the wind most often blows
**tropics**          warm area of the world on either side of the Equator

Every part of the world has a **prevailing wind**. This is the direction the wind most often blows.

In the tropics the prevailing winds blow from east to west. Near the North and South Poles the winds also blow mainly from east to west. In between these two places, the prevailing winds blow from west to east.

◀ The arrows show the direction that the world's prevailing winds blow.

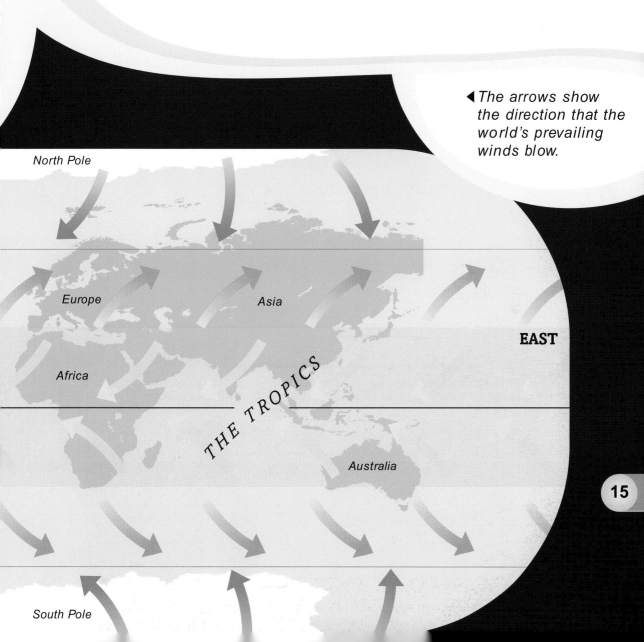

North Pole

Europe

Asia

EAST

Africa

THE TROPICS

Australia

South Pole

15

# Pirate attack!

Your ship has reached the **tropics**. The weather is very hot. In the tropics it is hot for most of the year. But near the North and South Poles it is cold all year round.

These places have very different **climates**. The climate is the general type of weather that a place has. The weather in a place can change from day to day. But over a long time, the climate of a place stays the same.

One of the sailors on your ship has climbed to the top of the mast. He sees a ship in the distance. The ship is sailing towards you. As it gets closer, the ship fires its cannon. It is a pirate ship!

## Pirate watch

*Pirates are people who attack and rob ships at sea. In the 1700s there were many pirates. The most famous were Blackbeard and Captain Kidd.*

**climate** general kind of weather a place has

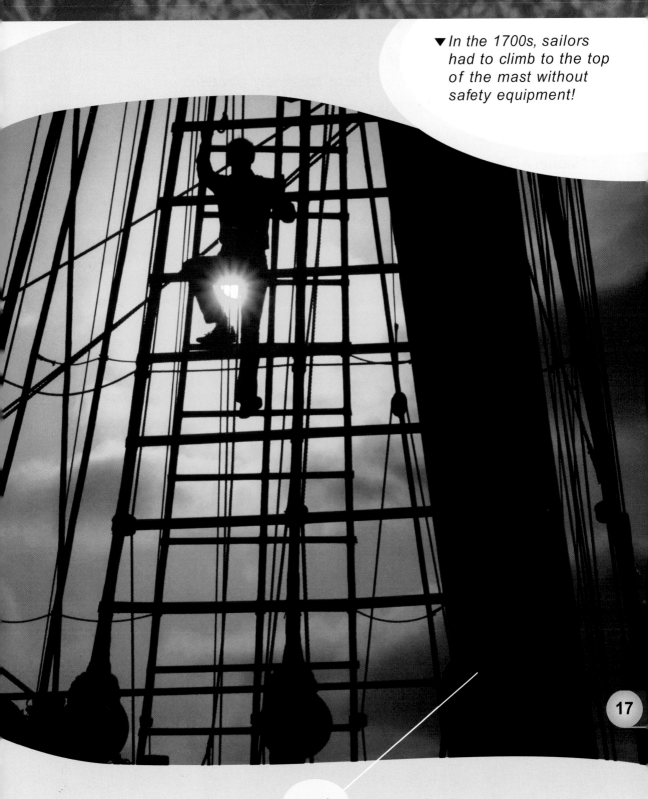

▼ In the 1700s, sailors had to climb to the top of the mast without safety equipment!

mast

# Captured!

The pirates attack your ship. There are many pirates. Their ship has many weapons. You and the sailors fight bravely, but it is soon over. The pirates make you their prisoners. They take you to the pirate ship.

The pirate ship is full of stolen treasure. For a week or more it is very hot. You and the sailors from your ship have to do all the worst jobs. Then one hot day you see some wispy clouds high in the sky. "Those clouds mean that it will rain soon," says one of the sailors.

In the 1700s sailors could **forecast** the weather by watching the sky. The different kinds of clouds told them if the weather was going to change.

## Cloud watch

Scientists have given names to different kinds of clouds.

- **Cirrus clouds**. These clouds often mean fine weather. They can also warn of a change in the weather.

- **Cumulus clouds.** These clouds mean it could be fine, or that there might be some light rain.

- **Stratus clouds.** These clouds mean it will rain.

- **Cumulonimbus clouds.** These clouds mean there may be a storm.

this photo are cirrus clouds.

cumulonimbus

cirrus

cumulus

stratus

# The weather changes

The sailor was right! Later that day the wind gets stronger. It begins to rain. At first the rain feels cool and pleasant. But soon it is raining heavily. You are soaking wet and cold. How can so much water fall out of the sky? Where does it all come from?

There is often heavy rain after many days of hot weather. The hot weather makes water **evaporate** from the sea. This means that the water turns into a gas called **water vapour**. The warm, wet air rises. As it gets higher it cools down.

Some of the evaporated water (gas) **condenses**. This means it turns back into water droplets. These water droplets form clouds. Soon the droplets in the clouds become too heavy to float. The droplets fall to the ground as rain.

| | |
|---|---|
| **condense** | when a gas turns to a liquid |
| **evaporate** | when a liquid turns to a gas |
| **water vapour** | water as gas |

▼ Water is always changing – from gas into water, then back to gas again. This is called the water cycle.

The Sun heats the ocean.

Clouds rise and cool. Water falls from clouds as rain.

Cooled water vapour condenses. It forms clouds.

Water vapour rises and cools.

Water falls on land. It flows down rivers and returns to the ocean.

Heated water evaporates (becomes gas).

# Hurricane!

The weather gets worse. The winds get stronger. The sails on the pirate ship are blown away. Huge waves crash against the ship. The storm has become a **hurricane**.

Hurricanes are huge, circular storms. Hurricanes happen in tropical areas. During a hurricane the wind can blow at 300 kilometres (186 miles) per hour.

The **air pressure** at the centre of a hurricane is very low. Air pressure is the weight of the layer of air around the Earth. Air rushes into the centre of the hurricane. This is because of the low pressure.

## Satellite watch

*Scientists use **satellites** to take pictures of hurricanes from high above the Earth. Then scientists can warn people who live in the hurricane's path.*

▼ The centre of a hurricane is called the "eye". The wind speed is lower in the eye of a hurricane. The sky is clear, but the sea remains very rough.

eye of the hurricane

There were many shipwrecks ▼ in the 1700s. This was often because ships had no engines, or weather **forecasting** equipment.

# Shipwrecked

Disaster! The strong winds of the **hurricane** smash the pirate ship on to some rocks. The ship sinks. The pirates escape in the ship's lifeboats. You and the other sailors are left behind.

You and another sailor grab a floating piece of the wrecked ship. You are very lucky. You are washed ashore on a desert island.

Islands have mild **climates**. This is because they are close to the sea. The weather on islands is rarely very hot or very cold. This is because the sea cools down and heats up more slowly than land. In summer, the sea is cooler than the land. Summers are not as hot near the sea. In winter, the sea is warmer than the land. Winters are not as cold near the sea.

# Modern forecasting

Luckily you are rescued from the desert island. You and the other sailor are the only ones who know where the pirate ship sank – with all the treasure!

Your pirate adventure is over. But just imagine if there really was treasure on a desert island! In a ship with an engine it would be much easier to sail there. Modern ships also have electronic machines to help them **forecast** the weather. It would be easier to avoid storms, too. There is only one problem. Where exactly was that desert island...?

*Modern ships have all kinds* ▶ *of equipment for weather forecasting. For instance, they can get warnings from weather* **satellites** *if a bad storm is coming their way.*

# Forecasting

## In the past...

People watched the sky and made up rhymes such as this:

*Red sky at night, sailor's delight.*
*Red sky in the morning, sailor's warning.*

This rhyme often works! When the sky looks red at sunset, it is because the sunlight is bouncing off dust in the air. Dry air traps a lot of dust. It can mean that dry weather is coming.

When the sky looks red at sunrise, it is because the Sun is shining on icy clouds to the west. These clouds can be a sign that rainy weather is coming.

# In the present...

Information about the weather is gathered by weather stations like the one in the photo. The weather stations measure wind, rain, and **air pressure**. The information is then sent from the weather stations to **satellites**. The satellites send the information to weather centres all over the world.

# Glossary

**air pressure** weight of the layer of air around the Earth.

**atmosphere** layer of air around the Earth.

**climate** general kind of weather a place has. The climate at the North and South Poles is cold all year round.

**condense** when a gas turns to a liquid. Clouds form when moisture in the air condenses into water droplets.

**Equator** imaginary line around the middle of the Earth.

**evaporate** when a liquid turns to a gas. On a hot day, water evaporates from the sea and rises into the air.

**forecast** work out what will happen in the future. Weather forecasters try to work out what the weather will be like over the next few days.

**gale** very strong wind. Gales are caused by air rushing quickly into places where air pressure is very low.

**hurricane** very powerful storm. The winds in a hurricane are strong enough to turn over cars and blow the roofs off buildings.

**offshore wind** wind blowing from the land out to sea. Offshore winds usually blow in the evening.

**onshore wind** wind blowing from the sea towards the land. Onshore winds generally blow during the daytime.

**prevailing wind** direction the wind most often blows. The prevailing winds are different in different parts of the world.

**satellite** machine circling in space above the Earth. Satellites have cameras and other instruments to see what is happening below. They can be used to forecast the weather.

**tropics** warm area of the world on either side of the Equator. The climate in the tropics is warm all year round.

**water vapour** water as gas. Water vapour is invisible. Clouds are water droplets that have condensed from water vapour.

# Want to know more?

## Books to read

- *How Weather Works*, by Michael Allaby (Dorling Kindersley, 1999).
- *The Magic School Bus Kicks Up a Storm: A Book about Weather*, by Nancy White, Joanna Cole, Art Ruiz (Illustrator) (Scholastic Paperbacks, 2000).

## DVDs

- *Wild Weather* (2002)
  A BBC documentary about extreme weather.

## Websites

- www.bbc.co.uk/weather/weatherwise has lots of facts about the weather.
- Learn about hurricanes, tornadoes, and other kinds of wild weather at skydiary.com/kids.
- www.miamisci.org/hurricane contains more about hurricanes from the Miami Museum of Science.

Find out more about the way that water becomes rain and snow in *The Life and Times of a Drop of Water*.

What would happen to the weather if the Earth stopped turning? Find out in *The Day the Earth Stood Still*.

# Index